Hello, Family Members,

Learning to read is one of the most important accomplishments of early childhood. **Hello Reader!** books are designed to help children become skilled readers who like to read. Beginning readers learn to read by remembering frequently used words like "the," "is," and "and"; by using phonics skills to decode new words; and by interpreting picture and text clues. These books provide both the stories children enjoy and the structure they need to read fluently and independently. Here are suggestions for helping your child.

- Have your child think about a word he or she does not recognize right away. Provide hints such as "Let's see if we know the sounds" and "Have we read other words like this one?"
- Encourage your child to use phonics skills to sound out new words.
- Provide the word for your child when more assistance is needed so that he or she does not struggle and the experience of reading with you is a positive one.
- Encourage your child to have fun by reading with a lot of expression . . . like an actor!

I do hope that you and your child enjoy this book.

　　　　　—Francie Alexander
　　　　　Reading Specialist,
　　　　　Scholastic's Instructional Publishing Group

Activity Pages
In the back of the book are skill-building activities. These are designed to give children further reading and comprehension practice and to provide added enjoyment. Offer help with directions as needed and encourage your child to have FUN with each activity.

Game Cards
In the middle of the book are eight pairs of game cards. These are designed to help your child become more familiar with words in the book and to play fun games.
• Have your child use the word cards to find matching words in the story. Then have him or her use the picture cards to find matching words in the story.
• Play a matching game. Here's how: Place the cards face up. Have your child match words to pictures, put cards face down. Have the child lift one card, then lift a second card to see if both match. If cards match, the child can keep cards. If not, place the cards face down once again. Keep going until he or she finds all matches.

*To my mother Angeline
and my sister Marica,
the gardening divas!*
—A.S.M.

To my reader, Nina
—J.D.

Text copyright © 1999 by Angela Shelf Medearis.
Illustrations copyright © 1999 by Jill Dubin.
All rights reserved. Published by Scholastic Inc.
SCHOLASTIC, HELLO READER! and CARTWHEEL BOOKS and associated logos
are trademarks and/or registered trademarks of Scholastic Inc.

Library of Congress Cataloging-in-Publication Data

Medearis, Angela Shelf, 1956-
    Seeds grow / by Angela Shelf Medearis; illustrated by Jill Dubin.
        p. cm. — (My first hello reader!)
    Summary: In simple rhymes, this book describes how seeds turn into sunflowers.
        ISBN 0-590-37974-7
        1. Seeds—Juvenile literature. 2. Germination—Juvenile literature.
    3. Plants—development—Juvenile literature.
    [1. Seeds. 2. Plants—Development.] I. Dubin, Jill, ill. II. Title. III. Series.
    QK661.M44 1999   98-23888
    575.6'8—dc21   CIP
                                                                          AC

10 9 8 7 6 5 4 3 2 1   9/9 0/0 01 02 03 04

Printed in the U.S.A.   24
First printing, April 1999

Seeds Grow!

by Angela Shelf Medearis
Illustrated by Jill Dubin

My First Hello Reader!
With Game Cards

SCHOLASTIC INC.
New York Toronto London Auckland Sydney

We plant some seeds
in the ground.

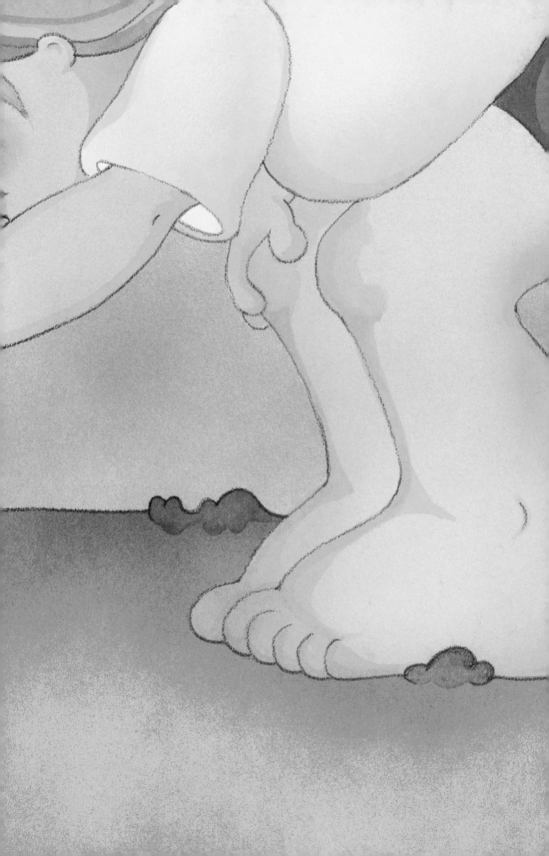

We sprinkle water
all around.

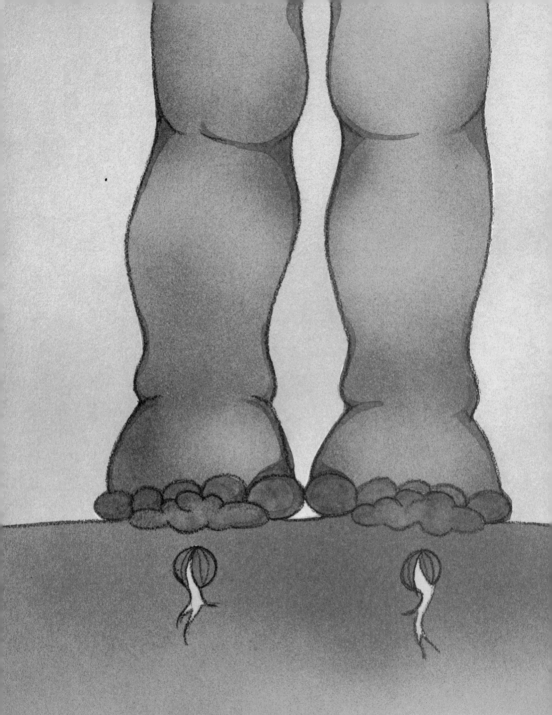

Soon roots push out...

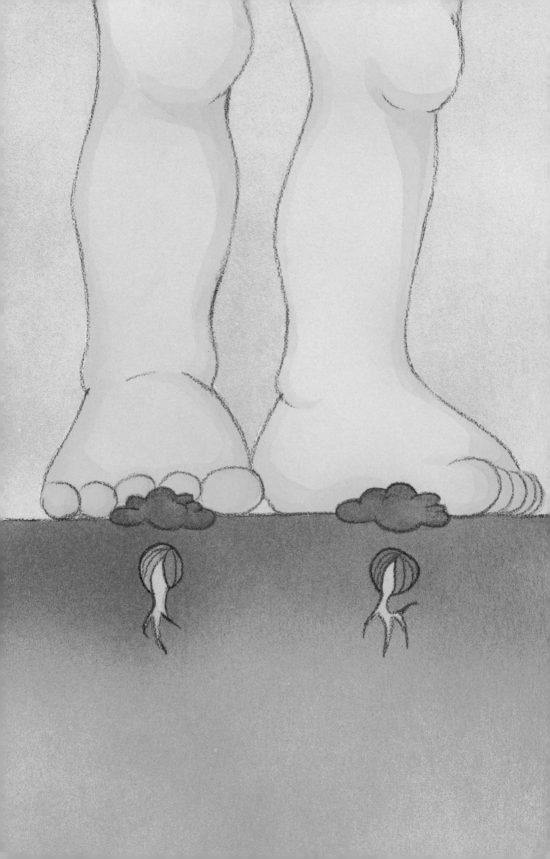

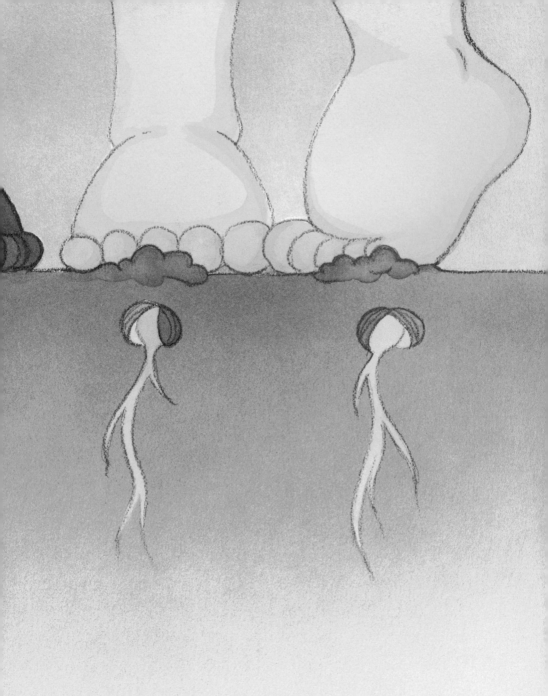

...and then down, down, down.

Little shoots
now come out.

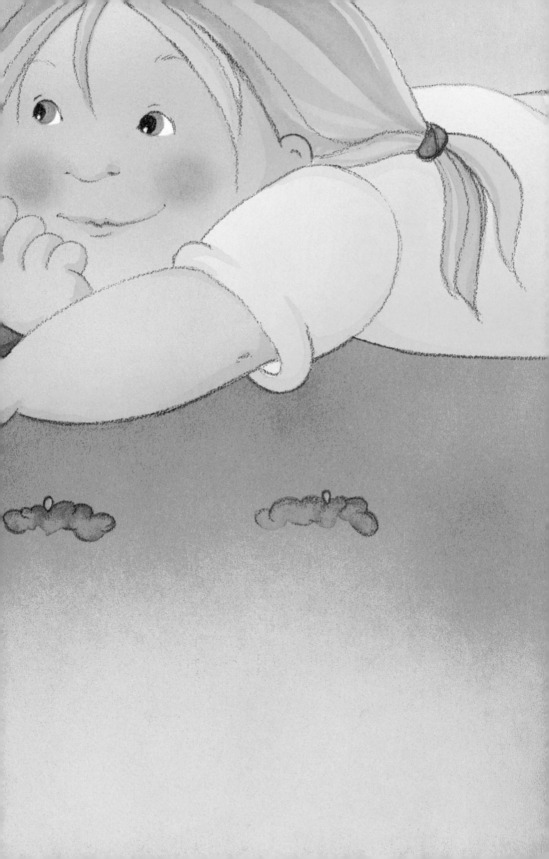

Then the shoots

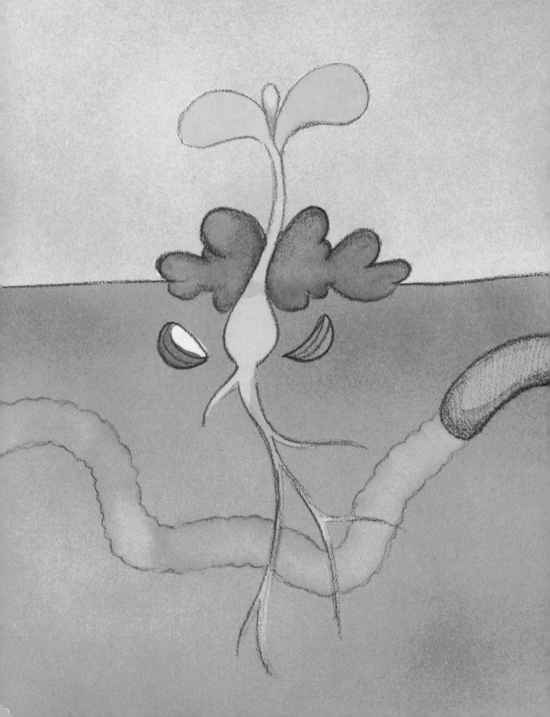

start to sprout.

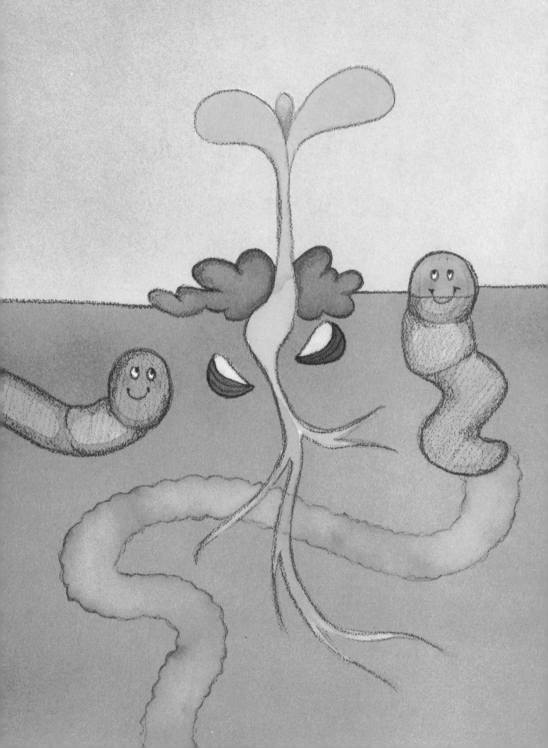

The leaves unfold,
one by one.

The buds grow up
toward the sun.

The petals unfold

and turn to gold.

Rain showers
water the flowers.

Bees buzz here
and there.

Sweet smells fill the air.
Pretty sunflowers
are everywhere.

Flowers, Flowers Everywhere

Match each flower to its color.

 **1.**   **orange**

 **2.**   **pink**

 **3.**   **yellow**

 **4.**   **red**

Opposites

Opposites are words that mean something completely different. For example, **right** is the opposite of **wrong**.

Draw a line to match each word with its opposite.

in	**down**
sweet	**out**
up	**pretty**
ugly	**sour**

Picture Perfect

Point to four things you would need to grow a flower.

Just for You

Connect the dots from **A** to **K** for a surprise.

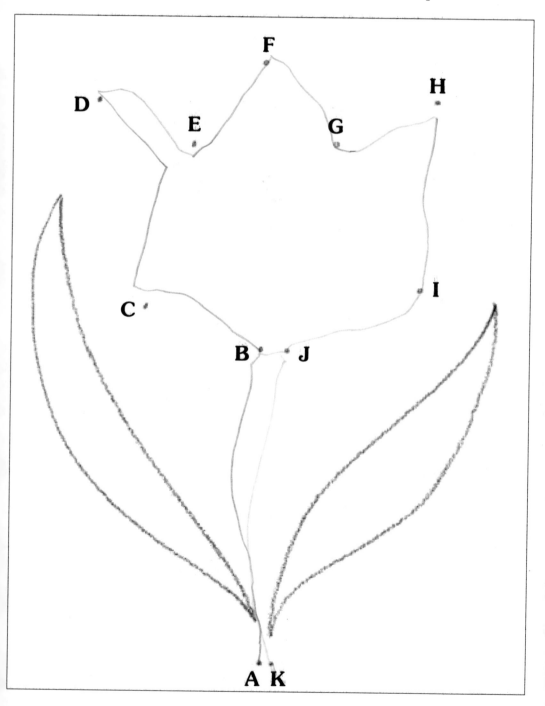

Rhyme Time

Sun and **fun** are two words that rhyme.
Point to the picture that rhymes with each word.

seeds

are

start

shoots

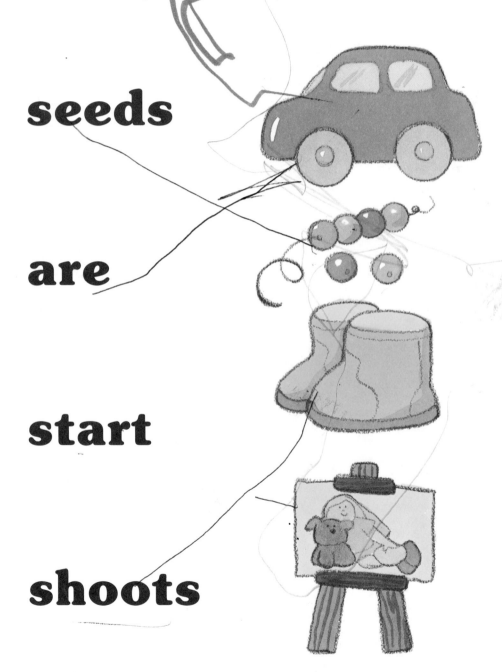

Art Fun

Use the space below to draw and color your favorite flower.

ANSWERS

Flowers, Flowers Everywhere

1. red   **3. pink**

2. orange   **4. yellow**

Opposites

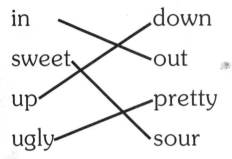

in — sour
sweet — out
up — down
ugly — pretty

Just for You

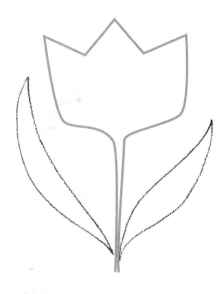

Picture Perfect

These are the four things you would need to grow a flower.

Rhyme Time

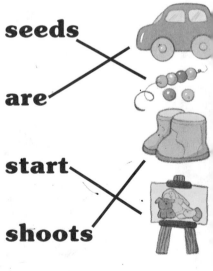

seeds — beads
are — car
start — art
shoots — boots

Art Fun

Pictures will vary.